GREAT TRANQUILLITY

Also by Yehuda Amichai

Songs of Jerusalem and Myself (1973)
Amen (1977)
Time (1979)
Love Poems (1981)

Yehuda Amichai

Great Tranquillity:
Questions
and
Answers

Translated from the Hebrew by Glenda Abramson
and Tudor Parfitt

1817

HARPER & ROW, PUBLISHERS, New York
Cambridge, Philadelphia, San Francisco, London
Mexico City, São Paulo, Sydney

Some of these poems have previously appeared in *The Times Literary Supplement, London Magazine, Ariel, Modern Hebrew Literature,* and *Jewish Affairs.* The following poems first appeared in *Poetry:* "Things That Have Been Lost" and "A Meeting with My Father."

FIRST EDITION

Designer: Sidney Feinberg

Library of Congress Cataloging in Publication Data

Amichai, Yehuda.
   Great tranquillity.

   Poems.
   Translation of: Shalyah gedolah.
   1. Abramson, Glenda. I. Parfitt, Tudor. III. Title.
PJ5054.A65S413   1983   892.4'16   83–47550
ISBN 0–06–015188–9   83 84 85 86 87 10 9 8 7 6 5 4 3 2 1
ISBN 0–06–091085–2 (pbk.)   83 84 85 86 87 10 9 8 7 6 5 4 3 2 1

Contents

8

GREAT TRANQUILLITY

Since then

I fell in battle at Ashdod
In the War of Independence.
My mother said then, he's twenty-four,
And she lights a candle of remembrance
Like birthday candles
You blow out on a cake.

Since then my father died of pain and sorrow
Since then my sisters married
And named their children after me,
Since then my house is my grave and my grave, my house,
For I fell in the pale sands
Of Ashdod.

Since then all the cypresses and all the orange trees
Between Negbah and Yad Mordechai
Walk in a slow funeral procession,
Since then all my children and all my fathers
Are orphaned and bereaved
Since then all my children and all my fathers
Walk together with linked hands
In a demonstration against death.
For I fell in the war
In the soft sands of Ashdod.

I carried my comrade on my back.
Since then I always feel his dead body
Like a weighted heaven upon me,
Since then he feels my arched back under him,
Like an arched segment of the earth's crust.
For I fell in the terrible sands of Ashdod
Not just him.

And since then I compensate myself for my death
With loves and dark feasts
Since then I am of blessed memory,
Since then I don't want God to avenge me.
Since then I don't want my mother to cry for me
With her handsome, precise face,
Since then I battle against pain,
Since then I march against my memories
Like a man against the wind,
Since then I weep for my memories
Like a man for his dead,
Since then I put out my memories
Like a man, a fire.
Since then I am silent.
For I fell at Ashdod
In the War of Independence.

"Emotions erupted!" so they said then, "Hopes
Mounted," so they said but say no more,
"The arts burgeoned," so said the history books,
"Science flourished," so they said then,
"The evening breeze cooled
Their burning brow," so they said then,
"The morning breeze ruffled their hair,"
So they said.
But since then winds do other things,
And since then words say other things
(Don't tell me I'm alive),
For I fell in the soft, pale sands
Of Ashdod in the War of Independence.

An Arab shepherd is seeking a kid on Mount Zion

An Arab shepherd is seeking a kid
on Mount Zion,
And on the opposite hill I seek my little son.
An Arab shepherd and a Jewish father
Both in their temporary failure.
Our two voices meet above
The Sultan's Pool in the valley between.
Neither of us wants the son or the kid
To enter the terrible process
Of the Passover song "One Kid."

Afterwards we found them between the bushes,
And our voices returned to us
And we wept and laughed deep inside ourselves.

Searches for a kid or for a son were always
The beginning of a new religion in these mountains.

Lying in wait for happiness

On the broad steps leading down to the Western Wall
A beautiful woman came up to me: You don't remember me,
I'm Shoshana in Hebrew. Something else in other languages.
All is vanity.

Thus she spoke at twilight standing between the destroyed
And the built, between the light and the dark.
Black birds and white birds changed places
With the great rhythm of breathing.
The flash of tourists' cameras lit my memory too:
What are you doing here between the promised and the
                    forgotten,
Between the hoped for and the imagined?
What are you doing here lying in wait for happiness
With your lovely face a tourist advertisement from God
And your soul rent and torn like mine?

She answered me: My soul is rent and torn like yours
But it is beautiful because of that
Like fine lace.

In the Old City

We are weepers at feasts, carvers of names on every stone,
Smitten by hope, hostages of rulers and history,
Blown by wind, inhalers of holy dust,
Our king is a sweet weeping child,
His picture hangs everywhere.
The steps always force us
To hop as if in a merry dance,
Even those who are heavy hearted.

But the divine couple sit on the terrace
Of the coffee house: he has a mighty hand and an
        outstretched arm
And she has long hair. They are calm now,
After a sacrifice of halvah and honey and the incense
        of hashish,
Both are dressed in long transparent robes
Without underclothes.
When they rise from their rest opposite the sun
Setting in Jaffa Gate, everyone rises
To look at them:
Two white halos around the dark bodies.

The eternal mystery

The eternal mystery of oars
that strike back while the boat floats forward,
thus actions and words strike back the past
so the body can move on with the man inside.

Once I was sitting in a barber's chair by the street
and in the large mirror I saw people coming toward me
and suddenly they were cut off and swallowed up in the abyss
beyond the large mirror.

And the eternal mystery of the sun setting in the sea:
even a professor of physics says:
Look the sun is setting in the sea, red and lovely.

Or the mystery of phrases like
"I could be your father,"
"What was I doing a year ago today?"
and other such words.

A meeting with my father

My father came to me in one of the intermissions
Between two wars or between two loves
As if to an actor resting backstage in half-darkness.
We sat in the Café *Atarah*
On Mount Carmel. He asked me about my small room
And if I was coping on my modest teacher's pay.

Daddy, daddy, before you made me you must have made
Cherries that you loved,
Black with so much redness!
My brothers, sweet cherries
From that world.

The time was the time of evening prayer.
My father knew I no longer prayed
And said, let's play chess
The way I taught you as a child.

The time was October 1947,
Before the fateful days and the first shots.
And we didn't know then I'd be called the generation of '48
And I played chess with my father, check-mate '48.

You can rely on him

Happiness has no father. No happiness ever
Learns from the one before, and it dies, without heirs.
But sadness has a long tradition,
Passes from eye to eye, from heart to heart.

And what did I learn from my father: to weep full and
                to laugh loud
And to pray three times a day.
And what did I learn from my mother: to close my lips, collar,
Cupboard, dream and suitcase, and to put everything back
In its place and to pray three times a day.

Now I have recovered from the lesson. The hair of my head
Is cropped, like a soldier from the Second World War,
Round and round, and my ears not only hold up my skull but
                the whole sky.

Now they say about me: "You can rely on him."
I've come to this! I've sunk this low!
Only those who really love me
Know you cannot.

In the mountains of Jerusalem

Here where a ruin wants
to be a building again, its wish is added to ours.
Even thorns are tired of hurting and want to console,
and a tombstone, torn from a desecrated grave,
is placed in the new wall with its name and dates,
happy that now it will not be forgotten.
And the children who alone could change everything
are playing among the rocks and the ruins.
They don't want to change anything.

Canceling a night of love in the Negev
makes a flower grow in the hills of Jerusalem,
things empty and fill up
but you are not always with the ones that fill up,
and the sage does not always assuage thirst
but tears a deep wound in forgetfulness,
evokes a memory of an old thirst.

Everything here is busy with the task of remembering:
the ruin remembers, the garden remembers,
the cistern remembers its water and the memorial grove
remembers on a marble plaque a distant holocaust
or perhaps just the name of a dead donor
so that it will survive a little longer than the names
          of others.

But names are not important in these hills,
like at the cinema, when the credits on the screen
before the film are not yet interesting and at the end
          of the film
are no longer so. The lights come up, the letters fade,

the rippling curtain comes down, doors are opened and outside
  is the night.

For in these mountains only summer and winter are important,
only the dry and the wet: and even people
are just reservoirs scattered around
like wells and cisterns and fountains.

The narrow valley

Young people picnic in the narrow valley
where I once fought a battle:
they camp next to the fear
and build a bonfire in the trenches of death.

The prettiest girl among them smoothes her hair
with a toss of her head
the strongest boy among them brings wood for the fire.
The shelling is going on
the explosive has changed for the better, a smell
of blossoming wild honeysuckle in the air and the sound
of a song.

In the evening, when they go,
the landscape straightens out:
the narrow valley will rise like a dent in a ball,
and the view will be smooth as oblivion.

A meeting of veterans of the Palmach*
in 1978 in Maayan Harod

Here at the foot of Mount Gilboa we assembled,
A meeting of sorcerers,
Each with the spirits of his own dead.

There were faces that only after a few days
Exploded with memory, in the blinding light
Of recognition. But it was too late
To say: it's you.

There were closed faces like the stuffed letter-box
Of people who have been away for a long time.
The weeping not wept, the laughter not laughed,
The word not said.

There was a path, at twilight, between the orchards
Lined by cypresses. But we didn't walk
Into the fragrant darkness that makes us remember
And makes us forget.

Like guests who linger at the door
After the meal, so we lingered thirty or more years,
Without the will to leave and without the power to return,
The hosts already asleep in their darkness.

Farewell the living and the dead together. Even
The flag at half-mast flutters joyfully
In the breeze. Even longing is a bunch

*Palmach: The commando units of the Israeli army during the War
of Independence.

Of sweet grapes from which they tread wine for feast
and festival.

And you, my few friends, go now
Each of you to lead his herd of memories
To pastures
Where there is no memory.

Air hostess

The air hostess said put out all smoking material,
but she didn't specify, cigarette, cigar or pipe.
I said to her in my heart: you have beautiful love material,
and I didn't specify either.

She told me to fasten and tie myself
to the seat and I said:
I want all the buckles in my life to be shaped like your mouth.

She said: Would you like coffee now or later
or never. And she passed me
tall as the sky.

The small scar high on her arm
showed that she would never have smallpox
and her eyes showed that she would never again fall in love:
she belongs to the conservative party
of those who have only one great love in their life.

Two fragments of the population explosion

Two fragments of the population explosion,
We met by chance. Tiny, torn fragments.
But with whole nights and shared sleep until dawn.

And what a beautiful house it was, like the House
of the Lord! You eat and drink
And remember only once a year to fast and lament.

We didn't know the melting power of tears
And the breaking power of laughter which grinds
Everything to dust.

Now we still can say: "Half a week,
Three full days, another four nights."

How poor in years and even days
Are those about to part but how rich
They are in minutes and seconds.

All these make a strange dance rhythm

As a man gets older his life becomes less dependent
On time passing and changing. Sometimes darkness
Falls in the middle of a couple's embrace by a window.
A summer love finishes while love goes on
Into the autumn, a man dies in mid-sentence
And the sentence remains on both sides, the same rain
Falls on the one who departs
And on the one who stays, or that
One thought is carried through towns, villages,
And many countries in the head of a traveler.

All these make a strange dance rhythm
And I don't know who is dancing to it
Or who is making us dance.

Some time ago I found an old photograph
Of a girl who died long ago and myself
Sitting together in a children's embrace before a wall
With pears climbing on it: one hand
On my shoulder, the other hand free, stretched out
To me now from the dead.

And I knew that the hope of the dead is their past
And their past is no more, for God has taken it.

A child is something else

A child is something else. He wakes up
in the afternoon: at once he's full of words,
at once he hums, at once he's warm,
at once light, at once darkness.

A child is Job on whom they've made their bets,
without his knowing. He scratches his body
for pleasure, there's no pain yet.
They're training him to be a polite Job,
to say "thank you," that God has given,
and to say "please" when God takes away.

A child is vengeance.
A child is a missile into the coming generations.
I launched it: I'm still trembling from it.

A child is something else: to glimpse through the fence
of the Garden of Eden in the rain of a spring day,
to kiss asleep,
to hear steps in the wet pine needles.
A child saves from death.
Child, Garden, rain and fate.

An appendix to the vision of peace

Don't stop after beating the swords
into ploughshares, don't stop! Go on beating
and make musical instruments out of them.

Whoever wants to make war again
will have to turn them into ploughshares first.

Things that have been lost

From newspapers and notice boards
I find out about things that have been lost.
This way I know what people had
And what they love.

Once my tired head fell
On my hairy chest and there I found my father's smell
Again, after many years.

My memories are like someone
Who can't go back to Czechoslovakia
Or who is afraid to return to Chile.

Sometimes I see again
The white vaulted room
With the telegram
On the table.

Flowers in a room

Flowers in a room are beautiful
Through their desire for the seed outside.
Even though they're cut from the earth,
And even though they're without hope,
Their useless desire adorns the room.
You too sit in my room, made beautiful
By your love for someone else.

I can't help you.
The happy ones wear a thin gold band in their black hair
And a mark of joy is on their forehead.
And a Greek looks with blue eyes
Into a dark thicket and is in the dream of a woman
Far away without his knowing.

I can't help you,
The way I can't help myself.

I also make square pictures
Out of round love that was without limit.

People in the dark always see

People in the dark always see those
In the light. This is an ancient truth, since the creation
Of sun and night, people and darkness and electric light.
A truth exploited by warriors
For an easy kill in ambush, a truth that allows the wretched
To see the joyful, and the lonely to see lovers
In a room gloriously alight.

But between darkness and light real life goes on:
"I've locked the door," you said,
An important and fateful phrase. The words are still
            in my memory,
But I've forgotten on which side of the door they were said,
Inside or out.

And from the one letter I wrote you
I only remember the taste
Of the stamp's bitter glue on my tongue.

The rustle of history's wings, as they said then

Not far from the railway track beside the painful post office
I saw a ceramic plaque on an old house, and I knew
That this was the name of the son of someone whose girl
        I took
Years ago: she left him and came to me
And the young man was born to another woman
And didn't know about all this.

Those were days of great love and great destiny.
The colonial power imposed a curfew on the city and
        confined us
To sweet love in a room
Guarded by well-armed soldiers.

I paid five shillings and changed my ancestral name
From the diaspora to a proud Hebrew name to match hers.

That whore fled to America, married someone,
A spice broker, pepper, cinnamon and cardamom,
And left me with my new name and the war.

"The rustle of history's wings," as they said then,
Which almost killed me in battle,
Blew softly over her face.

And with the terrible wisdom of war they told me to carry
My first-aid bandage right over my heart
Over the foolish heart that still loved her
And over the wise heart that would forget.

The Sufla spring in the mountains of Judea

I took two friends with me to find
The spring which once in days of dust and sorrow
Quenched my thirst. The pipes have since taken its waters
To well-ordered places for fair allotment
And the passing years have absorbed the smell of well-watered
        plants,
And the words that described them
Describe things hard and dead.

Caution! Nostalgic area!

It's so easy to create madness if you take away memory
From a man who is remembering
Or from someone looking at a view
The view he's looking at, from the speaker
The one he's talking to
Or from someone praying, his God.

We didn't find the spring,
But by the roadside we did find
Layers of rest: the rest of stone on earth, the rest of
        the head on the stone,
And the rest of the heavens on this tired head.

Caution! Nostalgic area!

A tourist

On a great rock by the Jaffa Gate
sat a golden girl from Scandinavia
and oiled herself with suntan oil
as if on the beach.

I told her, don't go into these alleys,
a net of bachelors in heat is spread there,
a snare of lechers. And further inside,
in half-darkness, the groaning trousers
of old men, and unholy lust in the guise of prayer
and grief and seductive chatter in many languages.

Once Hebrew was God's slang
in these streets,
now I use it for
holy desire.

An iron gate melts into evening

An iron gate melts into evening.
Salvation is near and far,
Like a tree to its roots that it will never see.

But the hand that remembers brushing tears from a cheek,
Does so on a dry cheek too
And on a table with its last crumbs.

And the hand that shakes dust from a coat
Does so although
It knows "unto dust wilt thou return."

And how do you explain the eternal order of a house.
And beside it a tree and beside the tree a woman?
But if you look back
The face there is once more the abyss.

There are candles that remember

There are candles that remember twenty-four hours a day,
It's written on them. And there are candles that remember
      eight hours
And there are eternal candles that ensure a man's memory
      to his sons.

I am older than most of the houses in this country and most
      of its forests
Which are taller than I. But I'm still the child I was,
Carrying a vessel of precious liquid from place to place
And taking care, as in a dream, not to spill it,
Afraid of punishment and hoping for a kiss when I arrive.

And there are still a few friends of my father's left
      in the city
Scattered like relics without plaque or legend.

I have a child of my old age who in the year 2000
Will be twenty-two. Her name
Is Emanuella, may God be with us!

My soul is experienced and built
Against erosion like mountain terraces. I am a man
      who holds on.
I am a middle man, a buckle man.

On the day my daughter was born no one died

On the day my daughter was born no one died
In the hospital and at the entrance
Was written: "Today *Cohanim* may enter."
And it was the longest day of the year.
Out of great joy
I went with my friend to the hills of *Sha'ar Hagay*.

We saw a sick, bare pine tree covered only with countless pine cones. Zvi said that trees about to die bear more cones than the vital ones. I said to him: that was a poem and you didn't realize it. Even though you are a man of the exact sciences you made a poem. He replied: And even though you are a man of dreams you made a precise little girl with all the precise instruments for her life.

Come with me on my last road

Come with me on my last road.
My last road may go on another twenty years
Or thirty, for you it's the first road.

You're young and I'm much older than you,
You're fresh and I'm out of the deep-freeze.

How hard they tried to come between us: your father came
At noon, my mother appeared in a dream at night.
Even winds tried to tear us apart
And olive trees, trees of peace,
Whipped our days with their rough branches.

We moved from place to place, we slept outside without walls
So they couldn't write about us
In their writing on the wall.

You said: Our pride is that we sometimes
Can do what we really want.

I said: We're a new commentary to the verse,
"To do that which is straight." Straight is short.
So come with me.

Return from Ein Gedi

From the green and hidden lushness of Ein Gedi
We returned to the hard city. I called you Rejah
After the Arab name of the wadi
And after the Hebrew word for yearning.
We came back to our empty room already let to others.
On the floor a torn mattress and orange peels
And a sock, a newspaper and other knives for the heart.

What did we learn at Ein Gedi? To make love in the water.
What else? That the mountains are more beautiful as
        they crumble.

Once more we looked out of the arched window
Together we saw the same valley, but each of us
Saw a different future, like two fortune-tellers
Who disagree with each other in a serious and silent
        encounter.

A day after we left thousands of years had already passed
The piece of paper on which was written "Same place
Tomorrow at seven" had yellowed and crumpled straight away
Like the face of a child born old.

Again love has ended

Again love has ended, like a successful citrus season,
Or like a season's excavations which unearthed
Troubled things that wanted to be forgotten.

Again love has ended. After they've demolished
A big house and cleared the debris, you stand
On the square and empty site and say: what a small
Site the house stood on
With all the stories and people.

And from the distance of the valleys came
The sound of a solitary tractor at work
And from the distance of the past the sound of the fork
Clattering on the china dish
Mixing and whipping the egg white with sugar for the child
Clattering and clattering.

I dreamed a dream

I dreamed a dream: in my dream seven maidens
fat and sleek came up to the meadow
and I made love to them in the meadow.
And seven skinny windscorched maidens came up after them
and swallowed up the fat ones with their hungry thighs,
but their stomachs remained flat.
I made love to them too and they swallowed me too.

But she who solved the dream for me,
the one I really loved,
was both fat and thin,
both swallower and swallowed.

And the day after her I knew
that I would never return to that place.

And the spring after her, they changed the flowers
          in the field
and the telephone books with all their names.

And in the years after her, war broke out
and I knew I would dream no more.

I sleep tonight to your memory

To the memory of Batya B.

I sleep tonight to your memory,
Although the dream will certainly not be about you.
You too have changed now from weighed to weighing
But we, the living, get lighter from day to day,
Only our thrashing about grows
And makes the scales tremble in vain.

I don't know if you will find there
What you sought
With your dark eyes, during your short life,
But I can promise you
That the search will go on, not like searches
For survivors of a shipwreck that cease
After a few days or weeks.

This summer I must again decide
How to exist: whether to be like hardy, closed up
Summer plants or like a watermelon exploding
With red lost joy.

Rest in peace. Your soul is returned
Like a surprise gift. You improved it a lot
Since it was given to you, you improved it without knowing
And angels will open the beautiful wrapping
Crying out in wonder to each other.

Rest in peace now: even the broken clock
Has one moment of grace every day
And truth.

In the middle of summer suddenly
a smell of rain

In the middle of summer suddenly a smell of rain:
A memory of what was and a prophecy of what will be.
But the middle of summer is empty.

As when you find a lost child
After a long search and the joy
Of finding him cancels the anger
And the rising anger destroys the joy,

Or like the sound of a slammed door
Some time after people have left,

Or like a man who holds out a woman's photograph
            to be punched
Instead of a ticket,
And he's let through.

A wedding song

Your parents supplied the woman and my parents the man.
God supplied the war and the ceasefire.
Carpenters cut four poles
And weavers wove the cloth for the bridal canopy.
But it billowed like a sail, tore loose and flew away.
And the poles are free now and beat us
And the foot goes on crushing glass after glass
And the hand tries to stick them together.

I ask myself, how long
Can you say "present" before saying
Book, watch, a pretty box?
And how long can you say "love"
Before saying he, she, them.

In a man's life his first temple is destroyed
And sometimes the second. It's not like
What happens to a people going into exile,
It's not like God who raises Himself up
From His ruined temple unto His heavens:
Man must always remain in his life.

An eternal window

In a garden I once heard
A song or an ancient blessing.

And above the dark trees
An eternal window is lit

To the memory of the face
That once looked out of it

Which too was in remembrance
Of another window lit.

Jerusalem is full of used Jews

Jerusalem is full of Jews used by history
Second-hand Jews, with small flaws, bargains.
The eye turns always to Zion. And all the eyes
Of the living and the dead are broken like eggs
On the edge of the bowl to make the city
Rich and fat and rise like dough.

Jerusalem is full of tired Jews
Always whipped into memorial days and feasts
Like bears dancing on aching legs.

What does Jerusalem need? It doesn't need a mayor,
It needs a ringmaster with a whip in his hand
To tame prophecies and to train prophets to gallop
Round and round in a circle, and to teach its stones
            to arrange themselves
In a daring and dangerous formation in the final act.

Afterwards they spring to the ground
To the sound of cheers and wars.

And the eye turns to Zion and weeps.

For ever and ever, sweet distortions

Pictures of dead Jews on the wall of a room in Petah Tikva,
Like stars that died eons ago
Whose light has only just reached us.

What's Jewish time? God's experimental places
Where he tests new ideas and new weaponry,
Training-ground for his angels and demons.
A red flag warns: Firing range!

What's the Jewish people? The quota that can be killed
          in training,
That's the Jewish people,
Which has not yet grown up, like a child that still uses the
Baby talk of its first years,
And still can't say
God's real name but says *Elokim, Hashem, Adonai,*
Dada, Gaga, Yaya, for ever and ever, sweet distortions.

Into an excavation

Into an abandoned excavation
There fell a small toy,
And while the child was still weeping
And the sound of his lament
Was reaching into the rest of his life, a thistledown
Prepared to hover over the dry lands.

And an aging teacher, who waited many years
For a girl to grow up
Is lying with her now, his mouth gaping like the dead.

An hour turns into a knife
To be used only once.

"Life will wipe that smile off your face,"
So they warned. "Time will wipe the tears
From your eyes," so they promised.
There will be many smiles left on time
There will be many tears smeared on life
Like on a good towel.

Song of love and pain

While we were together
We were like a useful pair of scissors.

After we parted we again
Became two sharp knives
Stuck in the world's flesh
Each one in his own place.

Dennis is leaving to bury his father

Dennis is leaving to bury his father.
For there are fathers who die alone and far from their sons,
And there are post offices where
There's more pain than in hospitals.

Dennis is leaving to bury his small, dead father,
For there are fathers smaller than their sons
(Once, while he was alive, he sat in my house
And his feet didn't touch the floor).

I saw a sign above a shop which announced
In big letters, Someone and Sons.
But I have never seen one that says, Someone and Fathers.
Maybe Jews are a business like this
"People and Fathers." Dennis too
Is "Dennis and Father."

Now he is leaving to bury his dead:
It's simple and clean, like in the Bible.

The parents left the child

The father and mother left the child with his grandparents,
Tears and pleading didn't work,
They went to enjoy themselves by the blue sea.

The grandparents' weeping has remained with them from
          before the Holocaust.
Sweet vintages of weeping.
The child's weeping is new and still salty,
Like the sea his parents are enjoying.

He is soon consoled: despite the strict rule
He sits on the floor and arranges all the knives
In meticulous order of size and type: the sharp, the serrated,
The long: a pain for everything
And a knife for every pain.

In the evening the parents come back
But he's already asleep in his deep bed.
He has already begun to be cooked in his life.
And no one knows what the cooking will do to him:
Will he get soft or harder and harder
Like an egg?
That's the thing about cooking.

Eyes

My eldest son's eyes are like black figs
For he was born at the end of summer.

And my youngest son's eyes are clear
Like orange slices, for he was born in their season.

And the eyes of my little daughter are round
Like the first grapes.

And all are sweet in my worry.

And the eyes of the Lord roam the earth
And my eyes are always looking round my house.

God's in the eye business and the fruit business
I'm in the worry business.

Spring song

In the morning I rise like a light plane
And look over my life: the old house, the smoke of
Burning leaven in the yard, the little girl who died
        afterwards.

At noon I land. The fragrant plane
Melts among flowering orchards.
I go on foot to a nostalgic encounter
Of the path with the road. A junction of remembering.
Names of bus companies that used to be:
"United," "Alliance," "Morning Star,"
All of them were full of promise
To stay together always.

There too is the tunnel of the thorny acacia
Blooming in fragrant yellow balls. I can crouch down
And go through it to my childhood
On the other side.

In the evening I choose brides for my sons,
Crazed with future I choose and choose
Everywhere, dozens of beautiful girls
Until I'm tired.

And at night a woman sings in the forgotten halls of life
"Once we didn't have to lock the doors at night,"
In a very sweet and lonely voice.

And I empty my body and say:
Come, peace, into my heart.

A gymnastics teacher from Petah Tikva

A gym teacher once lived in this deserted house.
Her skin was brown and soft as silk.
She reared a whole generation of hard stomach and leg muscles
for wars in the desert and for love among the orchards.

She herself left the country to live
in Vienna, the city of whipped cream. She left and got
      fat there.

On this spring evening I stand beside the house.
My knowledge of its imminent destruction
and the house's knowledge
that I will never come there again
together make a perfume stronger
than all the smells of war, and sweeter than the fragrance
      of orchards.

I came back once more

I came back once more to this place:
I remember it from the time when hopes
Still looked like the faces that hoped them;

But I didn't go into these rooms,
The windows broken, the screens torn,
And on the wall dates of other lives
And yellowing papers which announced
Battle orders and death.

The winds blowing now
Are the winds that blew then too,
But the noble voices that gave
Fateful tidings with quiet words have long been silent,
And the echoes are scattered over the whole land
As blessing or curse.

And the hopes that once looked like the faces of those
          that hoped,
Are now fewer and fewer
And are moving away, like these mountains,
Like these skies above the mountains
Which no longer seem like the face of anyone.

An attempt to hold back history

Next to the King David Hotel I saw ten respectable ladies
Lying on their backs across the road to stop
The Minister's vehicle on his way from the hotel to the house
    of destiny.

They screeched like excited pigeons, then cooed and cooed,
And pulled at their dresses so that their bare flesh
                wouldn't show.
I knew one of them. I put down my heavy baskets by her face:
Why are you lying here on the street, a respectable lady
In the process of divorce? Why are you lying happily on
            your back with your heavenly curls—
Embroidered fringes of destiny and
Ornaments for this difficult time? Do you think you can hold
    back history?

She didn't answer and I went my way.
But twenty handsome police cadets came
And carted them off:
Each of them was carried by two, like
Overripe fruit, into the police van. They screeched
Like excited pigeons, then cooed and cooed.

Sabbath lie

On Friday, at twilight of a summer day
While the smells of food and prayer rose from every house
And the sound of the Sabbath angels' wings was in the air,
While still a child I started to lie to my father:
"I went to another synagogue."

I don't know if he believed me or not
But the taste of the lie was good and sweet on my tongue
And in all the houses that night
Hymns rose up along with lies
To celebrate the Sabbath.
And in all the houses that night
Sabbath angels died like flies in a lamp,
And lovers put mouth to mouth,
Blew each other up until they floated upward,
Or burst.

And since then the lie has been good and sweet on my tongue
And since then I always go to another synagogue.
And my father returned the lie when he died:
"I've gone to another life."

Instead of a love poem

To Chana

From "thou shalt not seethe a kid in its mother's milk,"
They made the many laws of Kashrut,
But the kid is forgotten and the milk is forgotten and
         the mother
Is forgotten.

In this way from "I love you"
We made all our life together
But I've not forgotten you
As you were then.

Like a ship's captain

Like a ship's captain who, after the dinner party,
Shows his guests the engine room
In the bowels of the ship (beautiful women requested it)
And he takes them down the iron steps, opens
Doors with a clang and closes them,
And they stand marveling at all the shining
And the spinning and going up and down

In this way I show my guests my children's bedroom,
Open a door and close it quietly
And we hear three sorts of breathing
In different rhythms in the small room which is infinite.
And a faint bluish light shines above the door.

Beautiful are the families in Jerusalem

Beautiful are the families in Jerusalem:
A mother from a Russian curse, a father from a Spanish curse,
A sister from an Arab curse and brothers from a Torah curse
Sitting together on the balcony
On a summer's day in the scent of jasmine.

Beautiful are the houses in Jerusalem:
They are all mines on fixed fuses and therefore
There's no need to worry when you step on a threshold,
Turn the knob or shake hands.
If the time hasn't come there's no danger.

Yes,
Mr. Detonator,
Mrs. Coil,
Wick boy,
Fuse girl,
Timing device lads,
Always sensitive, so sensitive.

The child is sick

The child is sick. The rain that brought "blessing to
    the fields,"
Brought him sickness. He coughs at night,
His fever boils inside him like a kettle
And makes a warm house for the family.

He will ascend the mount of the Lord and I will come down
    from it,
He sustains distant candles with his breath.

I take his temperature.
I myself am like a thermometer:
Quicksilver inside and outside smooth and quiet.

The child is sick. I want to be
A young mother. I have to cross two barriers
For I am a father and I'm aging,
But I'll still make it,
If only I have the time.

In the morning it was still night

In the morning it was still night and lights were burning
When we rose from happiness like those who rise
     from the dead
And like them we immediately remembered our former lives:
That's why we parted.

You wore a striped shirt of old silk
And a tight skirt, an old-fashioned hostess of partings
And our voices were like loudspeakers
Announcing times and places.

Out of a leather bag, with soft folds like an old
     woman's cheeks,
You took out lipstick, passport, a letter, sharp as a knife,
You put them on the table
And you put them back.

I said: I'll move back a little like at an
Art exhibition to get a better view
And I haven't stopped moving back a little since.

Time will be light as froth,
The heavy sediment will stay in us.

In summer by the sea

In summer by the sea
God blows people up like rubber rings
And gives them summer souls
And makes them light.

At evening a full red sun stays
Like a ball of ice cream
Undiminished
But those licking it
Melt into darkness and oblivion.

And at night, huge neon letters
spell MEN WOMEN.

A young girl in the Negev

A young girl is sitting under
A lone tree in the Negev at noon.
She's waiting for a car. She's wearing
A very light dress, too short.

She's singing a song from the war:
The war is forgotten in the song,
And the dead are forgotten in the war.

And up to the horizon's edge the plain all around
Is covered with flint glinting in the sun
Like the eyes of a paralyzed old man
Following her—glinting.

Jerusalem ecology

The air above Jerusalem is saturated with prayers and dreams.
Like the air above industrial towns
It's hard to breathe.

And from time to time a new consignment of history arrives
And the houses and towers themselves are its packaging
Which is then thrown away and piled in heaps.

And sometimes candles come instead of men
And then silence.
And sometimes men come instead of candles
And then noise.

And in closed gardens, scented with jasmine,
Stand foreign consulates
Like evil brides that have been rejected,
Lying in wait for their moment.

The heavens are the Lord's heavens

The heavens are the Lord's heavens
And the earth He gave to man. But
Whose are the gold and marble houses of prayer?
And how many of the men who kiss the mezuzah
Have been kissed with a love like that by a woman?
And how many of the women who throw themselves
        on a holy tomb
Have ever been taken from behind and fainted from pleasure?

And what will become of the old tourist guide
Who's danced with Jerusalem since his youth.
Now he's tired but she carries on dancing
He's discarded at the gate
Trousers gaping with no buttons
And only flies still find him sweet.

The heavens are the Lord's heavens and the earth
He gave to man, but whose is the table
And whose is the hand on the table?

A memory in Abu Tor

There on the border stood an old hut
Half synagogue, half soldier's shower room
The tank up above, which supplied water
For the dust-covered bodies,
Supplied water for the ritual washing of hands too.
And through his water pipes, God on high supplied
Enough for them both.

A Sabbath hymn from below rose
With the shouts of hairy men in the showers.

The Lord is a man of war
His Name is the Lord of Hosts
The soldier is a man of youth
His name is engraved on a disc.

He who created man
And filled him full of holes*
Will do the same to soldiers
Afterwards, in war.

*The Hebrew refers to a prayer said after defecating, thanking God for having created man with orifices.

Tourists

Visits of condolence is all we get from them.
They squat at the Holocaust Memorial,
They put on grave faces at the Wailing Wall
And they laugh behind heavy curtains
In their hotels.
They have their pictures taken
Together with our famous dead
At Rachel's Tomb and Herzl's Tomb
And on the top of Ammunition Hill.
They weep over our sweet boys
And lust over our tough girls
And hang up their underwear
To dry quickly
In cool, blue bathrooms.

Once I sat on the steps by a gate at David's Tower, I placed my
two heavy baskets at my side. A group of tourists was standing
around their guide and I became their target marker. "You see that
man with the baskets? Just right of his head there's an arch from
the Roman period. Just right of his head." "But he's moving, he's
moving!" I said to myself: redemption will come only if their guide
tells them, "You see that arch from the Roman period? It's not
important: but next to it, left and down a bit, there sits a man
who's bought fruit and vegetables for his family."

The windmill in Yemin Moshe

This windmill never ground flour.
It ground holy air and Bialik's
Birds of longing, it ground
Words and ground time, it ground
Rain and even shells
But it never ground flour.

Now it's discovered us,
And grinds our lives day by day
Making out of us the flour of peace
Making out of us the bread of peace
For the generation to come.

The girl who worked at my bank has left

The girl who worked at my bank has left. Because of her
     great beauty
They moved her from window to window and from
     desk to desk
Until she went to study medicine in Italy.

When she was here I didn't know where she slept at night,
And now she's in Italy I certainly don't know.
But she will always be the tenant of her beautiful eyes,
And her two souls will remain fluttering in light despair
As if trying to escape from each other
But she holds them together with a strong metal clip.

The sleep I didn't sleep last night I want
To donate to her. So she can sleep quietly in her new place.
And although I only enjoyed her appearance
And the sight of her deft hands touching the little money
     I have
I want to say over her a blessing (even though
It's wasted), like the blessing over fruit, the blessing
Over fragrances, the blessing over miracles, the blessing
That he has given his beauty to humankind or that
     he has made
Everything with his word.
She too and her journey without return.

The creaking door

The creaking door
Where does it want to go?

It wants to go home
That's why it's creaking.

But it's at home!
But it wants to go in.

And be a table
And be a bed.

You mustn't show weakness

You mustn't show weakness
And you have to be tanned.
But sometimes I feel like the white veils
Of Jewish women who faint
At weddings and on the Day of Atonement.

You mustn't show weakness
And you have to make a list
Of all the things you can pile
On a child's stroller empty of children.

This is the situation:
If I take the plug out of the tub
After a pleasant and luxurious bath,
I feel that all Jerusalem and with it the whole world
Will empty out into the great darkness.

In the day I lay traps for my memories
And at night I work in Balaam's factories
Changing curse to blessing and blessing to curse.

And you mustn't show weakness.
Sometimes I collapse inside myself
Without people noticing. I'm like an ambulance
On two legs carrying the patient
Inside myself to a no-aid station
With sirens blaring.
People think it's normal speech.

Relativity

There's a toy ship with waves painted on it.
And there's a dress with sailing ships printed on it.
And there's the effort of remembering and the effort
        of blooming
And there's the ease of love and the ease of death.
A dog of four years equals a man of thirty-five,
And a day-old fly—a man advanced in years
And full of memories. Three hours of thought
Are as two minutes of laughter,
And a child crying gives his hiding place away in the game
And a silent child is forgotten.
Black long ago stopped being the color of mourning:
A girl squeezes herself into a black bikini
Cheekily.

A picture of a volcano on the wall
Soothes the people sitting in the room.
And a cemetery calms
By the quantity of its dead.

A man told me
That he's going down to Sinai because
He wants to be alone with his God:
I warned him.

We traveled unto a sleep far from us

We traveled unto a sleep far from us
So you would know, I would know, we would know.
We went into the evening, O beloved country.
A school trip wants to come to rest,
Houses of goodwill closed along the way,
Fires in the field were the start of a new religion.
Beside us a wise man sat silently.
Tears roll down the cheek,
Like a phone ringing in an empty house.

We were close to each other,
Like two related languages, like Hebrew and Arabic,
Like English and German.

We were good together, but your heart
Studied in a different school from your head.

Our meeting, in red joy, was illusory
Like the meeting of sun and sea at evening.

Straight from your prejudice

Straight from your prejudice you came to me
You hardly managed to get dressed.

I want to Judaize you with my circumcised body
I want to bind you in phylacteries from top to bottom.

I want to dress you in gold and velvet,
Like the Torah scroll, and to hang a Star of David around
        your neck.

And to kiss your thighs,
Like a mezuzah at the door.

I'll teach you the old custom
Of washing feet with love:

Oh, wash my memories for me,
For I've walked in them so much that I'm tired.

And my eyes are tired of the square letters of my language
I want letters that flow like your body.

I don't want to feel like a prophet of wrath
Or like a prophet of consolation.

I almost
Succeeded.

But when you cried, tears shone in your eyes
Like snow and Christmas trimmings.

You never grow up

You never grow up
Always tummy troubles and toothache
And dribbling feelings and garbled speech:
That was the crying of laughter. No,
That was the crying of crying.
He'll still learn to speak.

Through loneliness a carpenter will talk to a plank,
A man to his wife, a man to his friend or his God,
And even his wars he makes on himself.
His enemies have moved away.

The most you can do is walk against the wind and clouds,
And sometimes return to a place from which you've come
To reenact the trial.

Afterwards you're silent. But on all sides
Shouts multiply: Remember what you did in the
                summer of '58!
Explain what you said! You're
Lying! Don't do it!
Don't be a child.

Two girls live in an old house

Two girls live in an old house.
Sometimes they overflow and sometimes they vanish like
       streams in the desert.
Sometimes they're ten and sometimes they're just one.

Sometimes their yellow light burns all night,
Like a chicken battery for twenty-four hours of love
And sometimes there's only a small reddish light
Like a sweet with a halo around it.

A great mulberry tree stands in the middle of the yard.
And in the spring there's a lot of fruit on the tree
And on the ground.

One of them bends down to gather,
And the other stretches out to pluck.
My eyes enjoy them both:
One wears a man's T-shirt and nothing else,
The other, sandals with thongs
Wrapped round almost to the navel.

When I have a stomachache

When I have a stomachache
I feel like the whole world.
When I have a headache
Laughter rises in the wrong place in my body.
And when I cry, they put my father in a grave
Into earth that's too big, and he won't grow into it.
And when I'm a hedgehog, I'm inside-out:
The spikes grow inward and hurt.
And when I'm the prophet Ezekiel, I'll see in the vision
    of the chariot
Only the dung-covered feet of an ox and filthy wheels.

I'm like a porter carrying a heavy armchair
A long way on his back
Without knowing he can put it down and sit on it.

I'm like an old-fashioned firearm,
But accurate: when I love
The recoil is fierce, back to childhood, and painful.

I feel good in my trousers

If the Romans hadn't glorified their victory
With the Arch of Titus, we wouldn't know
The shape of the Menorah from the Temple.
But we know the shape of Jews
Because they multiplied unto me.

I feel good in my trousers
In which my victory is hidden
Even though I know I'll die
And even though I know the Messiah won't come,
I feel good.

I'm made from remnants of flesh and blood
And leftovers of philosophies. I'm the generation
Of the pot-bottom: sometimes at night
When I can't sleep,
I hear the hard spoon scratching
And scraping the bottom of the pot.

But I feel good in my trousers,
I feel good.

End of summer in the mountains of Judea

End of summer in the mountains of Judea. The land lies
As last year's rains left it. The firing range
        on the slope
Is now silent, riddled targets have stayed there
Like people. An old man cries out with gaping mouth
About the loss of land and flesh, and his small grandson puts
A round head on his knees without understanding
        what it's all about.

Further on pretty girls sit on a rock
Like severe lawyers
To protect the summer and administer its legacy.

Further on in a dark cave stands a fig tree,
The big brothel where ripe figs
Couple with hornets
And are split to death.

Laughter not burnt, weeping not dried,
And a great silence in everything.

But a great love sometimes starts here,
With the sound of dry branches breaking in the
        dead forest.

Glass and memory

Goodbye, grapes, until next summer.
The year will be very long. The wine
Made from you makes sweet forgetfulness, but you
Are sober and awake, glass and memory.

The earth's wisdom gathers moisture and sadness
While joy continues. Contracts
Of marriages in high places fly about,
And in the ancient winepress, hewn out of the slope,
Feet keep trampling even without grapes
Until blood spills over the hard stone.

Oh, gardens of longing, slopes of memory,
Houses of forgetting, little sarcophagi for small children,
A curl, a wheel and a spiral horn
And thin bones like the bones of a dove.

Goodbye, grapes. I don't know if
I'll be here next year but I know
That next year's grapes will be the same grapes:
Only people, heavy eyed,
Clumsy with pride and serious of soul,
Die, each one alone, with no return.

I don't know if history repeats itself

I don't know if history repeats itself
But I do know that you don't.

I remember that the city was divided
Not only between Jews and Arabs,
But between me and you,
When we were there together.

We made ourselves a womb of dangers
We built ourselves a house of deadening wars
Like men of the far north
Who build themselves a safe warm house
Of deadening ice.

The city has been reunited
But we haven't been there together.
By now I know
That history doesn't repeat itself,
As I always knew that you wouldn't.

A young girl goes out in the morning,
like a knight

A young girl goes out in the morning
Pony-tailed and swaying as if on horseback.

Dresses and handbags, sunglasses, chain and buckles,
Are like armor on her.
But beneath all this
She's light and slender.

Sometimes at night she's naked and alone.
And sometimes she's naked and not alone.

You can hear the sound of bare feet
Running away: that was death.

And afterwards the sound of a kiss
Like the fluttering of a moth
Caught between two panes of glass.

Closed are the doors

Closed are the doors that were to be
open to me forever. And those I can open
guard vacant places
like ancient despoiled graves.

I think about the love of people
who have forgotten
to take down decorations after the festival:
what do they have left?

Farewell to you too. The hour
we woke early to part
has stayed fixed in me, like an alarm clock
that needs to alarm no more, but just
clicks.

The playground

The trees in the playground grew or died,
And the children
Want to grow up at any price,
To get out and to love.

If you've seen a white curtain
Fluttering at an open window, you've seen
How people love.

If you've seen a barber sitting in a chair
In the evening and shaving himself at a mirror,
You've seen how people live.

If you've seen Jews standing praying for rain,
And pleading for rain in a rainy country,
You've seen how people remember.

If you've seen a child playing by himself
In the playground during the vacation
You've seen longing.

A second meeting with my father

Again I met my father in the Café *Atarah*.
This time he was already dead. Outside, the evening
Mixed oblivion and memory, as my mother
Mixed cold with hot in the bathtub.
My father hadn't changed but the Café *Atarah*
Had been renovated. I said: Happy are those
Who have a patisserie next door to a coffee house,
You can call inside: "Another cake, more
Sweetness, let's have more!"

Happy is he whose dead father is next door to him
And he can call him always.

Oh, the eternal scream of children
"I want, I want!"
Until it turns into the scream of the wounded.

O my father, chariot of my life, I want
To go with you, take me along,
Put me down next to my house
And then continue on your way alone.

We left. And a man remained in the corner,
One hand amputated.
(The last time he had two hands.)
And he drank coffee and put down the cup,
And ate a cake and put down the fork,
And leafed through a magazine and put it down,
And laid his hand on the magazine.
He laid it down and rested.

To forget someone

Forgetting someone is like
Forgetting to put out the light in the back yard
And leaving it on all day:
But it's the light
That makes you remember.

Great tranquillity: questions and answers

People in the painfully bright hall
Spoke about religion
In the life of modern man
And about God's place in it.

People spoke in excited voices
Like at airports.
I left them:
I opened an iron door over which was written
"Emergency" and I entered into
A great tranquillity: questions and answers.